OKOMI
Enjoys His Outings

Helen and
Clive Dorman

Illustrated by
Tony Hutchings

Dawn Publications
in association with The Jane Goodall Institute

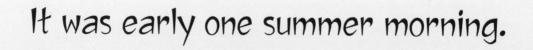

It was early one summer morning.

Okomi and his mommy,
Mama Du, were lying in their nest
enjoying a morning cuddle.

Mama Du gently scooped Okomi
from the nest onto her tummy
and swung down to the ground.

She was taking Okomi
on an outing.

Okomi was very excited.
He clung tightly to
Mama Du's hair with his tiny
hands and feet.

As Mama Du walked along
the path, Okomi swung gently
from side to side.

He thought this was
great fun.

After a while Mama Du
saw some fruit that had fallen
from a nearby bush.

She stopped walking and
sat down to eat.

Okomi watched his
mommy eating.

Okomi gazed around him
in fascination.

Everything Okomi looked at, every
sound he heard, and every smell he
sniffed, fascinated him.

Suddenly an excited
chimpanzee ran past them
waving a branch around
and hooting loudly.

Okomi was startled
and hid his head
in Mama Du's hair.

Soon it was quiet again
and Okomi looked around.

This time he saw a
brightly colored butterfly
fluttering about,
which made him laugh.

Okomi's large eyes
saw a tall, dark object which
went high up in the sky.

He followed it
to where there was a
strong bright light.

The shining light made him blink.

Okomi was looking at
a tree and the sun.

One day Okomi would be able
to climb right to the
top of that tree.

He would eat its
tasty new leaves and play
with its dry old leaves.

One day he would learn that
when the sun came up it was
daytime and time for play,
but when the sun went down
and the moon shone it was
night and time for sleep.

Mama Du gazed lovingly at
her Okomi.

As they continued
their walk, once again
Okomi clung on tightly to
Mama Du.

Each day Okomi
will discover something new
from his mommy.

She has many things to
teach him and Okomi has a
lot to learn about the
world in which he lives.

Enjoy your outings, Okomi!

Did you know?

Chimpanzees love to hug and kiss their friends and family. There are close bonds between family members. They are very intelligent.

When they are very young, baby chimpanzees cling to their mother's tummy. When they are about six months old, baby chimpanzees start to ride on their mother's back. At about the same age they start learning to walk and to climb trees.

Young chimps remain with their mothers until they are seven or eight years old. Chimpanzees in the wild can live for as long as 50 years.

Chimpanzees are our closest living relatives in the animal kingdom. These apes are found in the wild only in Africa. They share over 98% of their genetic material with us; they use and make tools; they express many of the same emotions that we do.

Fanni and her baby, Fax

Helping orphaned chimps

Jane with an orphan chimpanzee

Sadly, chimpanzee numbers are falling as their forests are cut down and they are hunted for the commercial bushmeat trade. This leaves hundreds of orphan chimps. An orphan chimpanzee can almost never be returned to the wild. Proceeds from the sale of each Okomi book supports the Tchimpounga sanctuary (in the Republic of Congo), where there are currently over 100 orphan chimps.

Roots & Shoots

One day in 1991, 16 students gathered on Dr. Jane Goodall's front porch in Dar es Salaam, Tanzania. They were fascinated by animal behavior and environmental concerns, but none of their classes covered these topics. They wanted to know how to help chimpanzees and other animals. Those 16 students went back to their schools to form clubs with other interested young people, and Roots & Shoots began. Since then, the program has spread rapidly throughout the world. More than 3,000 Roots & Shoots groups for children pre-K and up have formed in more than 68 countries around the world. There are many active groups in the U.S. and Canada.

Their mission is to foster respect and compassion for all living things, to promote understanding of all cultures and beliefs and to inspire each individual to take action to make the world a better place for the environment, animals and the human community. For more information contact the Jane Goodall Institute, P.O. Box 14890, Silver Spring, MD 20910, or call (301) 565-0086, or go to www.janegoodall.org.

Dawn Publications is dedicated to inspiring in children a deeper understanding and appreciation for all life on Earth. To view our full list of titles, or to order, please visit our web site at www.dawnpub.com, or call 800-545-7475.